To
Vince

THE COVE DIARY'S
ALMOST SERIOUS GUIDE TO SENNEN COVE

ANDREW CARNE

Best Wishes

Andrew Carne

May 2022

The St Ives Printing & Publishing Company

THE COVE DIARY'S
ALMOST SERIOUS GUIDE TO SENNEN COVE

© Andrew Carne

First Edition published 2017

Cover Photograph © Aerial Cornwall

Printed and Published by:
The St Ives Printing & Publishing Company,
High Street, St Ives, Cornwall TR26 1RS, UK.

ISBN 978-0-948385-87-2

Contents

Introduction

This guide is written for the broad-minded visitor who does not mind a bit of humour with his or her history and a fairly tongue-in-cheek approach to being guided about the little huddle of houses clinging to the cliff known as Sennen Cove.

Most of what you will read is, in fact, fact. It is just that the author could not help himself from adding one or two embellishments of his own. The whole purpose of this was to relieve the author of the fag of having to do research which, as we all know, can be time-consuming, irritatingly long-winded and most probably end up with being controversial.

Where I have been lacking in knowledge I have employed (and I use the loosest definition of the word) experts in the field, less to assure the correctness of the facts but more to help spread the blame. You will find that large portions of the text have been plagiarised. If you are the original author, first, thank you, and secondly there is no point in complaining as I admit it fully and therefore it would look vindictive, sour grapes if you were to sue.

Naturally any resemblance or reference to anyone living, dead or slightly poorly is entirely cheeky if not plain coincidental.

Acknowledgements

Shouldering some of the blame in this venture, whether knowingly or nor, are the Missus, largely for just being the Missus and for casting the first opinion on the draft and Rose Griffiths for the primary edits. Looking after the flowers was Karen Platt, the only proper expert in the whole book, who also provided some of the photographs. I also need to thank owners of the various businesses and, in one particular case the owner of a beach, for their kind input and promising not to take legal action.

The cover image is by Aerial Cornwall's Matt, who pulled out all the stops on an unexpectedly bright day in February to get the shot. Print and canvas copies are availble from his website, aerialcornwall.com

The map printed in this guide contains OS data © Crown copyright and database right (2016).

Overview, Orientation and a Little History

SENNEN COVE LIES ALMOST at the western tip of England, just a mile from Land's End. It sits in the old district or Hundred of Penwith, which itself means the land's end, roughly translated from Cornish language. After leaving Penzance, the largest town in West Penwith, follow the A30 trunk road for approximately eight miles. A traveller, who was not following an errant satellite navigation system, passes into the village of Sennen. Just past the school there is a turning on the right which leads down into Sennen Cove via Cove Hill.

As the road descends further, the huge vista of Whitesands Bay opens out with the collection of houses and cottages dispersed over the hill on the left and also below. Further down, as the footpath on the right peters out, more of the bay becomes visible, including the main beach on the right and, outside high water, Cowloe reef to the left. The road to the left, just below the brow of the hill, is Maria's Lane, which gives access to the houses at the upper part of the cliff. The houses along this road have spectacular views out across the bay and are commensurately priced.

At the end of The Cove is the large granite headland of Pedn-mên-du, topped by an old coastguard watch house. This huge mass provides the village with shelter from the prevailing south westerly weather and the full force of the Atlantic when it feels like throwing a few big waves our way.

Across at the other side of the bay is Cape Cornwall, topped by a mining chimney stack. Just off the cape are the two rocks of the Brisons, only one of which can be seen from The Cove.

In the Beginning

The very beginning of Sennen Cove was, in all likelihood, a bunch of people who could not be bothered to go the rest of the way to Land's End. It seemed to offer a bit of shelter from the elements, particularly the prevailing wind and rain from the south west, had a half decent access to the sea for doing things like getting something to eat and had plentiful access to fresh water that either fell from the sky quite often or cascaded down the cliffside in streams. Even when it was not raining there were, and still are, plentiful springs all along the cliff above The Cove.

This is not intended as a history book so I will spend scant time in the past. Suffice it to say that the first people came here a very long time ago. There is evidence along the cliff towards Land's End of Neolithic, Bronze Age and Iron Age activity including the easily identifiable outline of Maen

Castle, built between 800 BC and 400 BC. It is unlikely that the Iron Age in West Penwith lasted very long; a scratch on my van will rust as you watch it.

Whitesand Bay, named after the colour of the sand - yellow, is notable as the location for the departure of King Athelstan to the 'lands of Scilly', the arrival of King Stephen and then King John, after roughing up the Irish, and lastly Perkin Warbeck during the reign of King Henry VIII. Since then no one else famous has bothered, since the airports are probably more convenient and you do not usually get sand in your socks.

There will be a little bit of history here and there throughout this guide. Be careful, there may be an embellishment or two so I would not trust this shallow pamphlet as a basis for your offspring's school project, "what I did on my holiday".

Fishing
Notwithstanding the prehistory artefacts of Mayon or Maen Castle (see The Walk to Land's End for more information) and the like, The Cove community most likely started up around the industry of fishing. There was, and still is, easy access to the sea and the bay. Even today it provides a living for a handful of fishermen, handlining, potting for crab and lobster, seine netting and jigging for squid come the end of the season.

While there is evidence that organised and commercial fishing was carried out in The Cove as far back as the 17th century and probably much earlier as a form of subsistence, it developed into a proper industry during the late 18th and 19th centuries. Some of the buildings along the front and many around the harbour you see today are from this period.

During the heyday, large punts were filled with pilchards or sardines, as they are now marketed, from seine netting. Buildings sprang up to process this catch which were packed and salted down for transport. Some evidence of pilchard cellars is still visible under what is now The Little Beach House holiday let in the RNLI car park. These cellars extended up to where the Harbour Mews houses are now standing.

Today, a number of fishermen belong to a seine net syndicate and each spring a sharp watch is kept for the appearance of shoals of grey mullet. When the mullet are in the optimum position, in the harbour or close in on the beach, a rowing boat will take one end of the seine net around the shoal and back to the beach. As the tide falls the fish are trapped in the net. There is some controversy regarding this practice as the grey mullet have come in to spawn. However, seine netting has been going on for many years and the fish still return in great numbers, which suggests that no permanent damage is done.

Round House

Today the Round House is a busy gallery, owned by the St Aubyn Estate and leased to a local artist who also has a gift shop in the net loft area. It is situated at the end of The Cove above the Harbour beach. Its location alone indicates its connection to the fishing industry.

The Round House was built to house the capstan that is still in place on the lower level of the building. The gear was part of a pre-steam winding gear from a tin mine so represents an early example of recycling. It also points to the fact that every expense was spared in the provision of the facility. The capstan was used to haul the large wooden pilchard punts in and out of the harbour and was driven by a team of men. It did not always have a roof and the capstan was open to the elements.

As you can imagine, in foul weather or, indeed, under the searing heat of the summer sun, conditions at the capstan would not have been comfortable. The complaints of the capstan turners were largely ignored until the emergence of the Capstan Turner's Union in 1876 when the men called a strike in the middle of the busiest part of the pilchard season. With the livelihood of the Cover's in peril the powers that be very quickly agreed to put a roof on the capstan building, which is what can be seen today.

The listed building was converted to a gallery in 1983. The old capstan mechanism can still be seen, covered with a glass top, in the lower room. The upper room, now filled with works of local artists and gifts, was once the net loft. Access to the lower room is through a small doorway and steep steps, so mind your head and step. There are steep steps, too, into the net loft and neither entrance is ideally suited to wheelchair or less than able bodied visitors.

The Wharf & Harbour

To the west of the Round House is the old Wharf. Today it houses several buildings both old and new which are store rooms for the fishermen who ply their trade out of The Cove. One of the buildings houses a modern refrigeration and ice plant for the small industry carried out here.

The older buildings have been part of this industry for more than 100 years and would have acted as salt houses and pilchard cellars as well as net lofts and stores.

The harbour is a Trust Port, established by Parliamentary Order in 1907 and is run, managed and administered by Harbour Commissioners drawn from local harbour users and authorities. The area of jurisdiction extends from Aire Point to Little Bo rock, then down to the Irish Lady rock off Pedn-mên-du.

This is a working harbour and a dozen or so punts and other boats are hauled up on the slipway. In this modern age, the working boats are launched and recovered by the Harbour tractor, an activity which is largely restricted to the mornings. While fishing is mainly carried out from March to November each year as the weather and sea conditions permit, the boats can be working at any time of the year and visitors need to be aware of the activity around them.

The Harbour Wall

The harbour wall is another iconic structure associated with The Cove. It gives some protection to the fishing fleet from the prevailing westerly swell and, although not its original purpose, permits the Lifeboat to be recovered in more difficult sea conditions than would otherwise be the case. It was raised by public conscription in 1909. The enterprise was orchestrated by

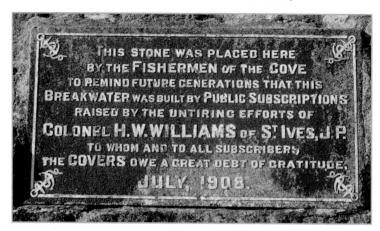

THIS STONE WAS PLACED HERE
BY THE FISHERMEN OF THE COVE
TO REMIND FUTURE GENERATIONS THAT THIS
BREAKWATER WAS BUILT BY PUBLIC SUBSCRIPTIONS
RAISED BY THE UNTIRING EFFORTS OF
COLONEL H. W. WILLIAMS OF ST IVES, J. P.
TO WHOM AND TO ALL SUBSCRIBERS,
THE COVERS OWE A GREAT DEBT OF GRATITUDE,
JULY, 1908.

Colonel H.W. Williams who led the call for funding and the whole enterprise took more than ten years in the planning and execution.

There is photographic evidence that prior to the current wall being built, a rough wall was in place constructed from piled up rocks. It lay in approximately the same position as the modern day wall but was not so high or so robust.

Sennen Beach Complex

For the want of a better name, the Sennen Beach Complex encompasses the restaurant that is run by the Michelin starred chef, Ben Tunnicliffe, the Beach Café and surf hire centre beneath it and the shop at the top of the car park that looks rather ecclesiastical.

Ben At Sennen

Ben Tunnicliffe took on the lease for the restaurant a few years ago and produces meals designed to cater for a wide appeal. Dishes are made using local ingredients wherever possible including a good range of fish caught in The Cove and from local suppliers. The menu is aimed at accessibility and surfers, walkers, cyclists and company are all welcomed. During the season there is a Surf Bar on the terrace which hosts summer evening entertainment.

The restaurant works with the neighbouring Sennen Surf School to put on competitions and events throughout the season.

Beach Cafe

The Beach Café is a kiosk arrangement that sits at the top of the beach, underneath the Beach Restaurant. It furnishes weary beach goers with pasties, drinks and sandwiches throughout the season. It is closed in the off season from October to April each year.

Sennen Surf Company

Newly reopened for the 2016 season, the shop sits in the Beach car park, looking much like a stylised church. This is no accident as it used to be called Chapel Idne (narrow chapel) after the old free chapel that stood nearby, the last remnants of which disappeared in 1946 according to record.

The new building has a Celtic cross in the window and is not particularly narrow but it is tall. The shop focuses on surfing products including wetsuits and accessories and surf boards. Downstairs is a range of surf orientated clothing as well as some beach goods.

Sennen Surf School

The school is closely associated with Sennen Surf Company where surf lessons can be booked and boards and wetsuits can be hired from the shop. The school has a long history at the Beach in Sennen Cove and runs from the beginning of April each year until the end of the October half term.

Both the Sennen Surf Company and Sennen Surf School operate under the banner of Sennen Surf Centre.

West Down Cove Road

As you reach the bottom of Cove Hill, the dominant form of The Cove's only public house and hotel, looms up on the left.

Old Success Inn

This was an old fisherman's inn dating from 1691 and up until the end of the 19th century was still a single, thatched building. It was added to piecemeal during the 20th century and now offers accommodation over fourteen bedrooms with an additional three separate apartments across its car park.

There is level access to the upper part of the bar area. Visitors with special requirements should visit the website or contact the inn directly.

The Old Success Inn was named, it is said, after a sailing vessel of the same name and is the only public house in The Cove. It offers meals at lunch and dinner and, at busy times, throughout the day. The Old Success featured in a contemporary 18th century text and explained that it was frequented by "blackhearts and ne'er do wells" and depending who you talk to, there has been little change. It was privately run until 2008 when it was taken over by St Austell Brewery.

The inn also boasts the only cash machine in The Cove, available during opening hours but this will not take overseas cards.

Cove Road

As you stagger out of The Old Success and turn left, you start to head along Cove Road. There are no street signs to tell you this but you may, should you desire, take the word of this pitiful journal and believe that it is, indeed, named thus. From here you can see the whole of the road stretched out before you, dominated by the Lifeboat Station at the end. Most of the buildings are 19th century, although there are some dating back much earlier.

Sunk into the middle of the pavement at this point is a line of mock canon bollards. These are largely to deter motorists from using the pathway as a car park. However, these are most useful in the pitch dark where the unwary can easily walk into them providing much merriment for partners and friends.

Wrest your eyes, for a moment, from the awe inspiring view of Whitesand Bay on your right and gaze to your left. As the wall of granite cottages breaks away up the line of Badgery Terrace, you will see a pair of metal tracks leading up the steep cliffside at the end of the row.

It is said that the original owner of the building above was obsessed with space and rockets. He built this launch ramp but unfortunately misjudged the angle, which accounts for the space beside the main house where the observatory used to be.

Of course, most people say it was a funicular installed to heave coal up to Carn North, the house above, and is a relatively recent – mid-20th century – installation.

Blue Lagoon Fish & Chips
The first shop you arrive at after leaving the Old Success Inn is the Blue Lagoon fish and chip shop. Understandably, it sells fish and chips and the usual additions but also provides cream teas and, according to the sign outside, locally caught crab sandwiches. There is seating inside and a small terrace in front of the shop if you wish to eat in.

Smart Surf School
The school operates all year round and is located adjacent to the Blue Lagoon Chip Shop. Smart Surf School provides surfing lessons for all abilities and offers a wide range of surf equipment for hire. It is a family business of local professional surfers including a British champion.

Little Bo Café

The café, down past the bus turning point and just before the Lifeboat station, has seen numerous changes over the last fifteen years. For the last five years or so it has been Little Bo Café and has carved a reputation for good, locally produced food and original dishes. The girth of the author of this guide can attest to the quality of the homemade cakes that are available daily.

Breakfasts are extremely popular as are the main meals through the day which are all homemade. The café is licensed and also provides a range of coffees and Cornish ice creams. There is limited seating inside but the café has further seating on the pavement opposite for the full al fresco feel. During colder days, blankets are provided for the less hardy diner.

Opening hours vary through the year, opening at 9 am through the main part of the season and slipping to 10 am in the shoulder months. Closing varies, too but mainly between 4 pm and 5 pm according to the season. The café is open during the off season but check ahead if you are planning visit during this part of the year.

The Old Boathouse Stores

This is a general store, gift shop, newsagent, grocery and off licence and is open throughout the season from the second weekend in March to the end of October each year. Hours extend for the summer school holidays and at Easter time but generally the shop opens at 8:30 am and closes at 6 pm.

The shop stocks a range of grocery products and, where possible, has a local focus such as bacon and other meats from a top St Just butcher, eggs, Cornish cheeses, Cornish butter as well as specialities like Cornish fudge, sweet and savoury biscuits and Cornish sea salt. Fresh fish can be ordered for next day delivery from Newlyn fish market, some of which is available from the shop's freezers.

As well as a range of gifts and souvenirs, the shop also stocks buckets and spades, beach equipment and a stock of affordable wetsuits and beach shoes. There is also a selection of clothes such as shorts and swimwear alongside towels, hats and hooded sweatshirts. Additionally some fishing tackle is available as well as a selection of preserved bait.

The shop doubles as the Sennen Cove Visitor Information Point with information on bus times, local attractions and directions and other enquiries a visitor may have.

Ice Cream Kiosk

Sited opposite the Lifeboat station is a small kiosk selling Kelly's Cornish ice creams, hot and cold drinks and pasties and sausage rolls to take away. There is also a range of inflatable toys to choose from as well as bodyboards. The kiosk is open during the season from mid morning to late afternoon.

Lifeboat

There has been a Lifeboat in Sennen Cove since 1853, a requirement highlighted by the wrecking of the *New Commercial* in 1851 on the Brisons, the large rock off Cape Cornwall to the north of The Cove.

In 1876 a new boathouse was built on the opposite side of the road, now The Old Boathouse Stores, and ten years later another bigger building was erected on the site of the original. The second slipway, the only Lifeboat station in the country to have two, was built in 1929. In its current form it permits the Lifeboat to be recovered at high water and in slightly more rough conditions than can be managed on the long slipway.

Since 2009, a Tamar class Lifeboat has been stationed at Sennen Cove, which also has a D-class rigid inflatable boat for inshore work.

There is a raft of history about the station, its boats and the people, which thankfully someone else has put in a book so this guide will not expand further. If you want to know more, buy the book, *Sennen Cove Lifeboats* by Nicholas Leach.

The Lifeboat is provided and run by the Royal National Lifeboat Institution, RNLI, which is a registered charity relying on public donations. The boats are crewed by a team of volunteers and ably supported by the very excellent Shore Crew who push the boat out and pull it back in when it returns.

There is a RNLI shop, contained within the building, selling Lifeboat oriented gifts and mementos. Next to the shop is a public viewing gallery from where the Tamar Lifeboat can be seen when it is in the station.

Beach Guide

"When we were here a couple of years ago there was a lovely big beach. Where is it now?"

It is easy to forget sometimes that those not lucky enough to live by the sea may not appreciate the workings of such things as tides that come in and go out and currents, which can spirit you away.

There are three beaches in Whitesand Bay, each with their own special character. Regular visitors will have favourites while others may change beach according to the weather, what the surf looks like or its dog friendliness.

Sennen Beach

This is the largest of the three and is about a mile long with largely soft, fine sand. The beach is L shaped, the main part running north-south and at the southern end, runs out to the west with varying amounts of sand turning to rocks about half way down its length. Its west facing appointment makes this a very popular surfing beach and attracts surfers from around the world all year round. It featured in *The Guardian* newspaper's "10 of the best surf locations in the world" alongside those in Bali, Hawaii and Portugal in 2016.

The main access to the beach is by the slipway opposite the Old Success Inn and this is also the emergency access for vehicles. Occasionally, such as in 2016, heavy seas removed the sand from the bottom of this slipway rendering it impassable to vehicles – and not much easier for people, either. Pedestrian access is available down slipways under The Beach complex. Additionally, there are steps from The Beach car park and half way along Cove Road opposite Blue Lagoon fish and chip shop.

During the summer months, and at other busy times through the year, this beach has RNLI Lifeguards in attendance. Swimmers and body boarders are urged to swim between the red and yellow flags for safety and surfers between the black and white chequered flags. It is ill advised to enter the water at all when the red flags are flying.

In the middle of beach, around 50 yards off the tide line at low water, lies the wreck of the SS *Beaumaris*. The tip of the binnacle can be seen on large spring tides poking out of calm waters. The two and a half ton tanker, only built in 1917, was torpedoed just north west of Longships in 1918. Most of the crew abandoned ship in the lifeboats and were guided to land by the then Sennen Cove Lifeboat, *Ann Newbon*. The captain, with the wireless operator, managed to beach the ship in the middle of the beach and is now a well know dive location.

Up behind the beach are grassy sand dunes. There is probably a scientific or proper name for the tough grass, my family used to call it cooch grass, but as this guide cannot be fagged with the research 'grassy sand dunes' is how it will stay, although there is a more informed entry in the Flora chapter. Half way along the beach is the entrance to

Vellandreath valley, where once the residents were known as 'sand fleas'. Today it is a verdant valley of holiday lets.

Nestled above the craftily hidden Second World War pill box to the north of the valley, on ground which is known as Carn Barges, are two black huts called Carn Keys, built in 1919 and used as a holiday home for the owning family.

At the northern extent of the beach is a rocky outcrop with a smaller beach (depending on the amount of sand about). The rocks are inventively named North Rocks and the beach set into them is Escalls Beans (pronounced Be-ans), meaning small, and also known as Little Gwenver to some.

From time to time during the summer various surfing competitions are held on the beach. There is also a very active Sennen Surf Club that involves the youth of the community, which meets on Saturday mornings during the season. The most iconic annual event is the Christmas Swim held on Christmas morning. In recent years, the annual, bathing suit only, dip has gathered momentum and regularly attracts between 200 and 300 swimmers. There is a gathering afterwards at the Old Success Inn where charity funds are raised for local concerns.

Sennen Beach Telegraph Cables

It is possibly an appropriate point in this guide to mention the part that Sennen Cove has played and continues to play in connecting the world telegraphically and, more recently, digitally.

The recent storms from 2008 to date have had the unfortunate effect of sporadically scouring out some of the sand from the beach. With the sand gone, cables can be seen, particularly at the bottom of the slipway opposite the Old Success Inn and, on occasion, more modern, steel encased cables have been revealed as they disappear into Vellandreath valley.

The first cables, the older ones at the southern end of the beach, were manufactured and laid by Siemens Brothers using Cable Ship Faraday around 1881 and leased by Western Union in that year. They run across the Atlantic to, initially Canso, Nova Scotia then, more latterly, to Bay Roberts, Newfoundland. Further cables were laid at this end of the beach up to the mid 1920s. The initial termination point was Cable Cottage, above where the Beach car park stands, and from here the cables ran to Alverton in Penzance, where Western Union had its office.

Gwenver (Gwynver)

Ordnance Survey has it named with a 'y', which is the old Cornish spelling but this guide has always known it with an 'e'. It is the beach that lies to the north of North Rocks and is privately owned but accessible to the public by kind, tacit, permission.

Again, the beach is blessed with light coloured, fine sand and many prefer this beach as it is quieter and more remote than Sennen Beach. The South West Coast Path runs into and along the back of the beach and, certainly at anything other than spring tide, low water, is the only direct method of access from Sennen Cove. When the tides are right, and there is plenty of sand about, the beach can be accessed from Sennen Beach, around or over and between North Rocks. Walkers need to be aware of the tide times and sea state before dallying too long on this short journey.

Alternatively, the beach can be accessed from the cliff behind the beach, where stone steps have been installed leading straight up the face. At the top, to the right, is a small car park provided by the beach owners which can be used for a small fee. To get there by road, leave Sennen village in the direction of Penzance, take the first turning left just after the sharp left hand bend at Escalls Chapel (the one with the surf board cross on the front). Follow the signs to Tregiffian until you come across a small round house behind the wall on the left. Here, take the entrance to the left for the car park. While you are here you might want to try one of Sarah & Finn's Awesome Brownies from the hut or maybe one of their excellent relishes.

Although it did not make *The Guardian* newspaper's list, some believe Gwenver Beach to be the better surfing beach. Indeed local comment has it that if there is no surf on Gwenver then there will be no surf anywhere else in Cornwall, as it is the first to benefit from the Atlantic swell.

There are no facilities on the beach at any time during the year, although Lifeguards patrol the beach at peak times.

Not to be outdone by Sennen Beach and on occasion, when enough sand has been scoured out of Gwenver Beach, the wreck of the *Trifolium* may be visible. This was an iron sailing ship on passage to Brazil when it came to grief on 10th March 1914. It had already interrupted its journey from South Wales to have leaks repaired at Falmouth but having left there, repaired, it hit a storm 50 miles off The Lizard. The heavy cargo of coal, bricks and clay shifted and the ship was blown, eventually, into Whitesands Bay and onto the rocks at Gwenver where the coastguard and crew failed to save her. The ship had only been renamed for this trip

which is considered unlucky, although leaking like a sieve and not strapping down your cargo is probably not going to improve your fortune. Six of the crew survived but the captain and one officer perished. This guide has been reliably informed that the ship's pig also managed to escape the wreckage and was taken in by a local farmer. The wrecking seems to have quite literally saved its bacon, as it was treated like a family pet thereafter.

We cannot leave Gwenver Beach without a mention of a grizzly find around five years ago of human remains, buried in the dunes. It is most likely that the bones were of a long dead mariner washed up on the beach prior to The Burial of Drowned Persons Act 1808. Before this date, drowned mariners were routinely buried close to where they were found. Following the wrecking of HMS *Anson* in Mounts Bay in 1807 and the public outcry of the number of bodies left on local beaches, a local solicitor, Thomas Grylls, drafted the act that stated drowned persons should be removed by churchwardens and buried in consecrated ground.

Harbour Beach

Lying under the iconic shadow of the Round House and between the Harbour wall and Lifeboat slipways, the Harbour Beach is often the quietest of the three. The sand is often a little more gritty than the other two beaches, although at the upper end it can be soft and white. It is also a working beach where the small Sennen Cove fishing fleet launches from, often early in the morning.

Due to its sheltered nature, the Harbour Beach provides a reasonably safe place for younger children to splash about in the water and, with due caution exercised, mess about on inflatable craft.

At low water it is a good starting point to investigate the rock pools and do a spot of crabbing. To the east, under the Lifeboat slipways, is a field of rocks to be explored, though foragers should mind their step as the rocks will be slippery. To the west, over the Harbour wall, is another stretch of rocks with deep gullies here and there; excellent crab country. As ever, make sure you check the times of the tides to ensure you are not caught out.

On high days and holidays, when the ground sea swell is breaking over the Harbour wall in huge, white cascades, the local dare devils will be out in force, lined up along the wall waiting to be swept away with the next big wave. While there is undoubtedly some risk involved in the practice, it is a rite of passage undertaken by most of the local lads, and maids. The Cove Diary has it on good authority that the 90 year old gentleman who lives along Cove Road used to do it when he was a boy.

Dog Days

Public Space Protection Orders dicate access to the beach for dogs during the year. Through the winter months there is a general free for all across all the beaches but between 1st May and 30th of September access controls are in force.

On Sennen Beach dogs are permitted before 8am and after 7pm. This restriction also applies to the Harbour Beach. It is a general rule in Cornwall that if a beach is difficult to get to, it is dog friendly. So it is with Gwenver Beach onto which dogs may be taken with impunity.

Angling

Throughout the year The Cove welcomes an army of keen sea anglers of all abilities. It should go without saying that standing at the margins of the ocean for any length of time is an inherently risky business. Before going anywhere close to the edge of the water make sure you know the tide times, the expected sea conditions and have the appropriate clothing and equipment, which in some cases may include a life jacket.

Some angling tackle can be purchased from The Old Boathouse Stores or there is a wider choice from West Cornwall Angling at the bottom of Alexandra Road in Penzance, including live bait.

There are a few favourite angling spots around the bay and in The Cove. The most regular is from the end of the Harbour wall. There is a sign on the wall to warn visitors off from walking on it. This is sound advice, especially when there is a large swell running; the waves will top the wall. Despite this, in quieter times, the far end of the wall is often used by anglers, although the rocky and weedy bottom here allows only spinning and float fishing or dipping with a crab line, perhaps. Using ledger rigs will only make the local shopkeeper happy when you keep going back for weights and hooks. Once, mackerel were abundant this close in but, more recently, small pollack, wrasee and garfish are more common.

Further along the rocks towards Pedn-mên-du there are deep gullies and less people. This area is only exposed at the lower reaches of the tide but anglers may expect to catch some pollack or wrasse from here, again using spinning rigs.

During the night, bright lights can be seen ranged along the main beach. These are not latter day wreckers plying their trade but sea bass fishermen, beach casting, and most probably local boys. During the high season, at least, it is unlikely that any beach casting could be achieved during the day due to the number of surfers, paddlers and general beach users. It would be advisable to check with the Lifeguards before attempting any beach angling during these periods.

For the more adventurous there is Aire Point on the other side of Gwenver Beach. While bottom fishing here is possible, great care should be exercised as even with a moderate swell, the waves will come crashing over the rocks. However, it seems that the smart money is in taking to the water in a kayak or small boat and fishing out in the bay.

7

Around Sennen Cove

It may stretch the imagination to consider that there may be any desire or necessity to leave The Cove at all during your visit. However The Cove Diary Guide understands man's basic instinct to explore his environment and reach beyond the boundaries of his known world. To this end, there follows a couple of classic walks that lead from the safe comfort of The Cove out into the wilderness of the Far West.

The Walk to Land's End

This sojourn is the one essential walk all visitors must complete at some point during their time in Sennen Cove. Some people will do this journey just the once while others will make it a tradition, completing the walk each year they stay.

Many visitors grandly announce that they are to set out on this epic journey and come prepared in big walking boots, rucksacks and provisions, should they require emergency sustenance en route. They are visually deflated when told that this is a straightforward amble of less than one mile, lasting no more than half an hour, if you take your time.

While it is a short and straightforward walk, it is not wheelchair friendly and only the lightest of pushchairs should be transported thither – or pedal driven fire engine if its owner is adamant and prepared to make enough fuss that it should go too.

The hardest part of the journey is the walk up the hill to the old coastguard station, which stands like a miniature castle overlooking the vista from Cape Cornwall to Land's End Point. It now is a National Trust

entrapment, erm, recruitment point manned throughout the season from Easter to the end of September or until the NT volunteer is blown out by an unseasonal gale. In any case, there is a well maintained stone path, courtesy of the National Trust, leading up the way, where care should, nevertheless, be taken as the stones can be uneven as stones often are.

Beside the lookout building is the support for a flagpole; the flagpole is put in place during the kinder months of the year. The flagpole was restored to operation in 2012 to celebrate 50 years of Royal Marine training in the area, as a plaque in front of the lookout details. Today, the Royal Marines still host the Mountain Leaders' course in the area, entertaining military from several countries as they send their top performers to hurl themselves off the top of Pedn-men-du, only to climb back up it again. They can also be seen, near naked, running down Cove Road, holding lorry tyres or bags of wet sand above their heads; ladies have been known to swoon. The Royal Marines flag is hoist up the flagpole whenever they are training as a warning to young ladies to avert their gaze.

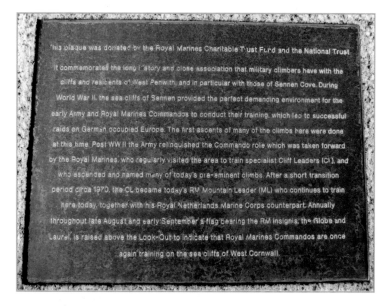

From the headland, Land's End can generally be seen, unless it is misty, in which case stand on the landward side of the lookout with it on your right and you are roughly heading in the right direction. Walk forwards carefully and whatever you do, do not turn right! The walk is relatively easy with only gentle and long inclines on the undulating route. The walk is gentle enough and, although this guide has seen young ladies complete the feat in heels, we feel that this cannot be recommended; stout shoes are probably better.

Along the route there are a few Iron Age artefacts such as the burial mound, now a few well ordered stones on the brow on the hill about

100 metres from the lookout. Further along, on the right of the path, is the National Trust marker for Maen Castle. Before you get to this point, the clear remains of the fortification wall can be seen climbing up from the mouth of the Castle Zawn.

At the bottom of this zawn, since 2003, is the wreck of the RMS *Mulheim*, which failed to turn to starboard at the appropriate time at the top of the, then, Traffic Separation System and bumped into the rocky bit called the coast. There is not much left of it now, torn to pieces by the power of the Atlantic storms over the years - the ship, not the coast, of which there is plenty, which was relatively undamaged by the incident.

As you approach Land's End, and we will not dwell on the attractions there, as they are well documented elsewhere, there is evidence of more modern building on the left of the path. There, broken brickwork and concrete plinths are the only remnants of RAF Mark's Castle, a Chain Home radar station from the Second World War.

For some variety, the return journey, if indeed you had intended to return, can be achieved back along the cycle path. This was constructed around ten years ago to provide access for, oddly enough, cycles and is also a bridle way. It also provides a convenient alternative for pushchair pushing parents and wheelchairs, although, for the latter, be prepared for a few pot holes and strenuous upward slopes.

The path commences (or ends) close by Land's End main entrance to the site. It takes a circuitous route around the border of cultivated fields and the rough moorland west of them. The path pops out at the end of Maria's Lane that runs the length of the cliffside between Cove Hill and Mayon Cliff, at the end of which sits the lookout. If you are a wheelchair user you will probably require a lift from here as there is no particularly easy route, depending on your capabilities, back down to Sennen Cove.

The Walk to Sennen Village

It may be hard to believe but it is possible that the facilities in Sennen Cove may not be able to fulfil your every need. There are additional services available in Sennen village at the top of the hill, such as a larger store and post office, a fish and chip shop, the Anglican church and another ale house, the famous First and Last Inn. There is also a motor repair business and, further towards Land's End, a holiday park and campsite.

Those with vehicular transport need only drive to the top of Cove Road and turn right toward Land's End, alternatively catch the right bus to arrive at these venerable establishments. Those on foot and relatively fit may wish to hoof it and for this purpose a well worn path exists between The Cove and Sennen (Mayon) Village.

Start out from the RNLI car park opposite the Lifeboat Station, the one with the barrier across the entrance. Strike diagonally across this to the right and you will pop out at the bottom of Stone Chair Lane. Turn left and go up the hill.

It is called Stone Chair Lane because it is a lane and has a stone 'chair' half way up. The chair is a large rock that sits to the left of the path as you ascend and harks back to the days when the men folk of The Cove were

exceptionally tall and not very fit and needed somewhere to sit on their way up the hill. You, dear visitor, being a sight more fit than our predecessors, will probably eschew use of the chair, particularly as it is around ten feet high. A more convenient bench is located at the top of the incline with views out across Whitesands Bay.

Having caught your breath and had it snatched away again by the breath-taking view, you will want to continue your journey up the path to Maria's Lane. On the opposite side of the road you will see a driveway to Esther's Field cottage. Approach and you will see that the footpath continues to your left and leads around the thatched cottage to a granite stile, the first of three you will encounter on this part of the path.

The remainder of your journey is unlikely to need further description as there is a metalled path across the field to the next stile. It then continues at the border of two fields, broken by another stile, until you reach the main A30 road, opposite the convenience store and post office. To the right there is the chip shop, Churchtown Village Hall, St Sennen Church and the First and Last Inn public house. Further down the road is Seaview Holiday Park and, at the end of the line, the Land's End attraction.

Sennen Farmers' Market

Since we are at the top of the hill it is worth mentioning at this point the award winning Sennen Farmers' Market. This runs on a Tuesday morning each week from around 9am to 12pm. It has won many awards during its existence most recently the Cornwall Food Awards, Gold Medal in 2016.

Here you may find green grocers, a fish monger, a butcher, an artisan baker and the occasional candlestick maker with various other local producers of both food and non-food products. It should be noted that not all the producers attend every week.

8

Flora & Fauna

Sennen Cove is visually a different place from time to time throughout the year. In spring and summer the wild flowers brighten The Cove in little nooks and crannies and everywhere you look there is a mass of colour. Come autumn some colours fade but golds and browns replace them. Then, in winter, it can be bleak with sharp greys setting off crashing seas and leaden skies.

The Cove Diary Guide has not the first notion what half the plants and animals are called but fortunately we have friends who do. Often there is a merging between the domestic and the wild, hereabouts, as the local bird population and strong winds have a habit of spreading seeds around.

Three-Cornered Leek/Garlic

The *Allium triquetrum* is bountiful in spring over much of Cornwall, where once you could be fined for growing it, as it is very invasive. So called, because the base of the leaf and the stem are triangular in cross section and when crushed it has the aroma and taste of mild garlic; it is sometimes referred to as tri cornered garlic. In The Cove you will find it growing all over the place and in hedgerows wherever you go during springtime.

The best thing about it is that it can be eaten from stem to flower and will compliment salads. The flowers can be pickled and the whole plant can be boiled or fried and preserved in oil and is known throughout Western Europe.

Chrysanthemum

No, not a wild plant but grows wild in The Cove – where else? At the end of Old Coastguard Row, alongside the steps leading up Mayon Cliff, there is a small semi-cultivated triangle. Here there are a couple of chrysanthemum plants quite happily flowering year after year with no interference at all.

Michaelmas Daisy

Another apparently domestic plant, the *Aster amellus*, can be seen in late summer, blooming away at the Harbour car park fringes, up along Old Coastguard Row and on Stone Chair Lane.

Sea Mayweed

Also on the margins of roads and all along Cove Road on the sea wall this bright flower can be seen for most of the summer and into autumn. *Tripleurospermum maritimum* if you wish.

Tree Mallow

The sturdy, *Malva arborea* (also known as *Lavatera arborea* or more recently as *Malva eriocalyx* – surely one name is enough) can be seen at all times during the year dotted about The Cove.

It is native to coasts of Western Europe and the Mediterranean and can be annual, biennial or perennial, growing up to two metres in height. The seeds, particularly, are edible, although the leaves are a bit furry. The plant was used in the 19th century as animal feed. The leaves also have been used in herbal medicine to treat sprains and burns. It sprouts blooms in mid to late summer of dark pink or purple flowers.

Gorse

The evergreen spiny shrub *Ulex europaeus* grows along the clifftops, its yellow flowers brightening up The Cove from April to June and sporadically at other times of the year. It releases a coconut scent that fills the air on a still day.

Hottentot Fig

Carpobrotus edulis is only really included because it has such a great name.

The only example in The Cove overflows the Cornish hedge surrounding Lewcott Cottage, but an example of its invasive credentials can be seen at Priest Cove, Cape Cornwall.

Spanish Bluebells

This interloper, *Hyacinthoides hispanica*, can often be seen amidst the three cornered leeks, particularly prevalent in the beds beside the steps leading up Mayon Cliff. The leaves are broader than the native bluebell and the flowers are arranged around the stem, as opposed to being clustered at the top. They are also a less intense blue and have no noticeable scent.

Montbretia

The flower seen growing over half of Mayon Cliff as you walk up to the lookout on Pedn-mên-du is an invasive hybrid, *Crocosmia x crocosmiiflora*. Early in the year it lights up the cliffside in luminous green as the sunlight shines through the leaves. When in flower, there is a carpet of red and green, a colour blind person's nightmare.

Marram Grass

This grass, the one that has a habit of catching your legs with its grey green slightly prickly leaves, colonises the dunes behind the big beach. Also known as the European Beach Grass, *Ammophila arenaria* has long roots that reach deep under the surface of the sand. Ladder like structures of underground stems, or rhizomes, extend

widthways from the roots capturing and stabilising the sand so the plants work hard in the war against erosion by the windy conditions prevailing here. This is a xerophytic plant which means it has adaptations to help prevent moisture loss. Its leaves curl inwards to minimise evaporation and the tiny hairs along their length cut down the air flow that could carry moisture away.

Red Campion

Is dotted around The Cove but most notably along Stone Chair Lane and the public footpath at Escalls Cliff. *Silene dioica*, sometimes flowering side by side with bluebells, usually comes into flower just after the bluebells have finished. They provide a pop of colour among the steely greys, greens and blues that prevail in the surrounding landscape.

Borage

The herb *Borago officinalis* has naturalised where the public footpath at Escalls Green joins Sunny Corner Lane. Traditionally used for medicinal and culinary purposes this soft grey/blue clump contrasts with the harsh strap like leaves of the surrounding *Phormium tenax* (New Zealand Flax). The plant smells faintly of cucumber and the flowers make a colourful addition to salads and cocktails.

Blackthorn

Also known as Sloe, *Prunus spinosa* grows prolifically in dense thorny thickets between the public footpath joining The Cove to Land's End and the cycle path that runs parallel to it. The timber is hardwearing and tough and was traditionally used for making walking sticks and tool parts. It burns well, and is often used as firewood. The sloes can be used for wine making, preserves and for flavouring gin.

Thrift/Sea Pink

Armeria maritima is a compact plant forming dense evergreen tufts of green linear leaves above which long stalks holding pink cup shaped flowers appear in May and June. It sometimes flowers again in September and October. Seen hugging the grassy slopes and rock crevices around The Cove, this delicate looking little plant is actually pretty tenacious and thrives in windy exposed sites with good drainage.

Some Birds

The Cove is alive with all manner of birds the whole year through. This guide can name a few but many do tend to look the same as others. Quite often, 'twitchers' will descend upon The Cove in numbers which is a sure sign that something interesting and rare has turned up. Perhaps the oddest was a Dalmatian Pelican, which arrived in 2016 and caused great consternation, not to mention a temporary 30 percent increase in population.

The Chough, the red beaked and legged crow type bird that sits on Cornwall's crest, and was missing from these shores for decades. They can now be seen quite commonly along the cliffs surrounding The Cove but never down amongst us.

There is also the occasional Wagtail hopping around quite unperturbed by passers by and the infrequent sighting of a Turnstone or two, pecking away at the paving stones but these are rarities. Following are some of the more common sights across the bay.

Oyster Catcher

Black and white sea birds with a distinctive call. It is a chubby little bird with long pink wading legs and a long reddish-orange beak for picking at its favourite meal of cockles.

Gannet

Large sea bird often seen diving from height, plummeting into the sea to catch fish. Adults are white with black wing tips and a pastel yellow head when seen close up. These birds are known to travel hundreds of miles to feeding grounds. Since there are no major nesting sites in our part of Cornwall, it is likely that the gannets seen in Whitesand Bay are from Wales or further.

Cormorant

There are a few of these about in The Cove. Black with long necks and can sometimes be seen drying their wings by extending and looking like they should be pinned to some heraldic shield. They are expert fishers and will dive from sitting on the surface, disappearing under the waves for some time before emerging with a fish hanging from its beak.

Tern – Common & Artic

Small birds, largely white with black cap, generally seen in the summer. They are most often seen in pairs as one good tern deserves another. Another has been known to constantly tell jokes – a funny tern, obviously, as opposed to its brother who is known for his short admonishments; a sharp tern. There have been rumours of big drug parties, not leaving one tern unstoned. The Cove Diary loves this bird for its pun value alone.

Gulls

There are all manner of gulls seen in The Cove at all times of the year. Predominantly Herring Gulls, Common Gulls, Great and Lesser Black Backed Gulls, Fulmar (not a gull but looks like one) although rarities can be seen from time to time and identifiable by lots of people in waterproofs, sporting long lens cameras and high powered field scopes wandering about looking excited. At least the gulls of The Cove are slightly more polite than those of our neighbouring towns and will ask politely for your ice creams and pasties rather than using menaces, fisticuffs and direct action to obtain them.

Jackdaws

Jackdaws can be seen in good numbers throughout The Cove. Largely black with a grey-blue collar and a stumpy black beak they are quite gregarious birds and we often see a sizeable group in and around the village. There is one resident who leaves seed out in his utility room and the birds are comfortable dropping by to feed. One, name Jack for some reason, became so domesticated that it would sit on his shoulder as he went about his wanderings.

Dolphins and Basking Sharks

Throughout the year the bay is visited by pods of Dolphins. These arrive without notice so it is no use asking, "What time do the dophins come in?" They are often seen close in, cavorting in the surf.

Basking Sharks are a little more erratic visitors lately; they used to arrive in great numbers during May and June. However, if you do see a dorsal fin cruising the bay, it is more likely to be a Basking Shark than Great White.

9

Where to Stay

This chapter is not intended to be a definitive list of accommodation in the area nor is it an exhaustive list. The Cove Diary Guide has just set out some of the larger facilities to provide some indication of what is available. It will be up to you to do your research to ensure that you do not end up sleeping under the stars when you rather expected to have a roof over your head or the bed you have paid for actually included a mattress as well.

As already mentioned, The Cove is a hotbed of holiday lets. These generally are rented out on a weekly basis, although out of season you may find some willing to do deals on shorter stays. One of the best places to look for accommodation is the Cornwall Far West website (www.cornwallfarwest.co.uk) where holiday lets and bed and breakfasts are listed from across West Penwith. Internet searches will, no doubt, provide alternative listings.

The Old Success Inn has already been covered in some detail earlier in this guide and is the only hotel in Sennen Cove itself. There is more limited accommodation also at Pengelly House, towards the Lifeboat Station end of The Cove. Other than self catering, these are the only regular short stay facilities in Sennen Cove.

The nearest camping and caravanning site is at **Trevedra Farm**, close to the A30 turn off for St Just on the road out of Sennen to the east. Here, there are good facilities including showers, a camp shop and café.

Follow the St Just road for the **"Sennen Cove" Camping and Caravanning Club** site at Higher Tregiffian. DO NOT follow your satellite navigation system, which will lead you to Sennen Cove itself and into a pickle about how to turn your caravan around on a narrow, busy street. Also, do not be tempted to drive through to the Harbour car park, as the tight corner is difficult, to near impossible, to navigate from the other direction.

Seaview Holiday Park sits at the west of Sennen village and offers static caravans, pine lodges and tent pitches with the new additions of "Glampods" and "Ecopods", according to its website. The campsite has an outdoor swimming pool, café and indoor facilities and entertainment for adults and children.

It would be sensible to check ahead as some of the facilities in the various campsites will only be available during the main season.

Accommodation of differing types are available at **Whitesands Lodge**, at the eastern edge of Sennen Village. Slightly to the west of this, on the A30, is **Sunny Bank House** offering six bed and breakfast rooms.

Both locations have websites with further details.

Sennen also has modern transport links further afield to places such as St Just and Penzance.

10

The Mundane Stuff

So as we come to the end, where you can breathe a sigh of relief and ponder regretfully the emptiness of your wallet, here is the boring, yet, oh so useful, stuff.

Being Prepared

The modern day Sennen Cove is a popular holiday destination. Most of the houses in The Cove are let out as self-catering accommodation and there are scarcely more than ten families who live permanently in the remaining houses. Within a mile or so of The Cove there are three camping and caravanning sites, including a Camping and Caravaning Club site on the road to St Just.

There are two main car parks and a small number of cafés, shops and restaurants. There is an hotel which also doubles as the only public house. Not all these facilities are 'card friendly' and before you visit you should be in possession of real cash money; at the very least you will need to park if you have driven here. There is a cash machine at the pub and at least one shop offers 'cash back' on purchases. Currently this only applies to UK cards.

Other access to cash, and particularly for foreign visitors, is thin on the ground. The nearest bank telling machine is at St Just in the wall outside the post office or in the Londis store in St Buryan. If you have the right brand of card, cash is also available in the local post office located in the Costcutter store on the main A30 in Sennen village.

Due to the holiday destination nature of The Cove, many businesses will not be open until near to Easter each year and will close in the autumn. Those that are open are likely to offer limited hours or service. It is best to check before you book, to avoid disappointment.

Waste Collections

The much maligned council contracts a company to collect waste on its behalf. In The Cove this happens on a Tuesday morning. If you are staying in a holiday let then you are likely to have a wheelie bin, which is good. Originally residents were told that all rubbish should be placed in a bin liner or refuse sack as it would be hand collected and that the wheelie bins would not be tipped as the lorries did not have this facility. Fortunately this turned out to be poppycock and wheelie bins are routinely tipped, although if the bin contains an easily lifted black bag the refuse operatives – or whatever their official title is – will lift this out because it is easier.

Using refuse sacks alone is not the greatest plan unless you do not mind holding it and waiting for the bin men to take it off you. Lone refuse sacks left for more than a nanosecond are fair game for the gulls hereabouts, followed by the jackdaws, wagtails and ground based scavengers. Soon there will be little evidence of any refuse sack and the non edible remnants of its contents will be randomly spread about the place.

Recycling

The much maligned council has an interesting attitude to recycling. It has removed many of the recycling points around the county and there are none whatever in or near Sennen Cove. It is the belief of the much maligned council that the little coloured bags and one green box delivered to each household in 2009 would be sufficient for eternity, ignoring the fact that the county's population increases three fold during the summer and not all these will be staying in households with pretty coloured bags – assuming anyone can remember what each colour is for.

If you are lucky enough to be staying somewhere with coloured bags they are collected fortnightly. Which week is which should be available on the much maligned council's website or by asking at The Sennen Cove Visitor Information Contact Point in The Old Boathouse Stores.

Public Toilets

There are public toilets each end of The Cove in the car parks. These are currently free to use. The Harbour car park toilets are maintained by Sennen Cove Harbour Commission and, currently, the Beach car park toilets are run by Sennen Parish Council.

In the Beach car park, alongside the main toilets, is a disabled toilet facility.